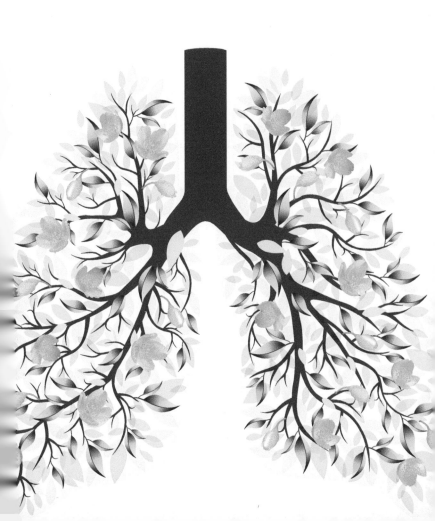

Also by Fiona Larkin

POETRY:

A Dovetail of Breath (Rack Press, 2020)

VITAL CAPACITY

Larkin

Fiona Larkin is a poet of close attention. In *Vital Capacity* she contemplates breath in all its variations, and examines the hidden trauma of tuberculosis, finding new ways to re-imagine the body - a chest is 'tight as the coat of a bud,' an exhaled breath hardens to 'a blown-glass prayer.' Her poems move gracefully between forms as she presents the personal and collective legacy of TB with empathy and imagination.
— Kathryn Simmonds, *The Visitations*

Powerful, inventive and immersive, *Vital Capacity* showcases Fiona Larkin's talent for making the most resistant materials shine, in a voice that is always compelling, compassionate and real. This is a perfectly poised collection which stays the course and maintains focus even when most of us would look away. Frequently heartbreaking in its combination of our silences and elisions with the kind of radical candour only poetry really gives us.
— Luke Kennard, *Notes on the Sonnets*

Larkin explores our relationship to disease, the body and our very essence. Her poems are absorbing and lyrically present. In this current climate Larkin's *Vital Capacity* creates a new myth and metaphor for our need to keep breathing.
— Jessica Mookherjee, *The Tigress*

ISBN: 978-1-915079-08-4

Cover designed by Aaron Kent

Edited and typeset by Aaron Kent

Broken Sleep Books Ltd
Rhydwen,
Talgarreg,
SA44 4HB
Wales

Contents

Vital Capacity

Fiona Larkin

Tuberculosis

let's obscure our troubles
blur sources
sluice closets
store our losses close to us

curious soloist   I rise
utter stories
elicit lilies
bisect / bruise / bless our tribe

Waking to the News

There is a kind of pain called exquisite,
a kind of curiosity called morbid.

To touch the wound is to probe
the border between sense and damage,
to test whether blunting is felt.

There is a kind of waking
when the head's night-long weight
presses ear to sheet

and each amplifying curve
expands into bruise.

Phthisis

def: Tuberculosis, esp of the lungs.

This is — what? A lisp, as if the tongue
has lost its nerve, grown to fill the mouth.

This is, perhaps, an ivied word
half in love with easeful… but

defies any glamorous decline,
any refining of the body, though

this is, it's true, a wasting of the flesh.
A shrinking back to bone.

This is not Camille, nor Violetta,
no Marguerite, nor any flower

but safflower, madder, walnut husk:
a foraging for hope.

This is a shroud for silence,
an erotics of shame, the stigma

of a lover named *Blauer Heinrich*
(a sputum flask in cobalt glass)

a whisper from the whistling chest,
a liquefaction of the lung.

This is a burning as the drowning starts.

This has acquired a new expression:
this is multi-drug-resistant.

This is, this remains,
almost unspeakable.

Tree Lungwort: a Taxonomy

dum spiro spero

pulled to heartwood
pulmonaria

lush, this lichen
algae-licked

paralleled
by lobe or lung

pleas for healing
bead each leaf

while I breathe I hope

Breathalia I

trachea

piper
inhale   tune your
instrument and rehearse
breath's song   chest's metronome rises
                      and falls

How to Ration New Medication

These (the Irish) patients
are temperamentally
undisciplined
from the point of view
of taking drugs

and also racially
they are very susceptible
to the disease

the intelligence
of many of them

often women

who are procreating
children at a vast rate

is low

and they literally
have not time
to take

or appetite for
these drugs

My Parents' Admissions

I leant too close, inhaled it from my patient.
        I breathed it in at seminary prayers.
                We met at a dance.

A cough that failed to leave, a wheeze.
        I hacked into my handkerchief.
                We met at a dance.

I recognised those caverns on my X-Ray.
        I hoped for Streptomycin, wonder drug.
                We met at a dance.

Instead, a state-run sanatorium.
        Another green hill, far away.
                We met at a dance.

They collapsed my lung, to let it rest.
        They left me with a dorsal scar.
                We met at a dance.

We ignored the morgue, discreetly out the back.
        A waltz supplied light exercise.
                We met at a dance.

In Which I Give Thanks For My Father's TB

seminary issue your bible   black-bound
         on the fly-leaf your confirmation saint

I don't know the candle of vocation   can't trace
         you very young black-quiffed emigrant

did you write of London's blessings   sing
         breathe on me breath of god in harmony

you inhaled the ghost   and were consumed
         coughed until the blood appeared

an L-shaped scar   across your back
         a piece of you that didn't fit

your damaged lung a map   of altered callings
         in sanatorium rural exile

breathe in the scent   of apple apricot
         light a candle for another love

and write to her with your given name

Tracing the Night

After the clocks have gone back
she wakes naturally, fast
emptying of dream.

She pushes back the heavier cover,
lifts the blind, and her usual view's
a blur of spherical pixels,

arcing up to the top frame,
roofs and plane trees nebulous
despite the morning brightness.

Each exhalation, each plume
of dream, has drifted, to layer
its print of alveoli on the pane.

Condensed, a night of breaths.
Each twitch, each depth, each gasp,
is made visible for an hour.

A bead of water melts into another:
she inclines, and sips
each slipping drop.

Breathalia II

pleura

salt-wash
store   gathering
in the margins   chorus
of sting and sweet   ambivalence
                    of tears

This is not a letter ...

... it is a kind of intake of breath before I begin
as if I were writing to someone in the air —

here, in two days, it is autumn
not late autumn, but bright gold everywhere

a real little salon with velvet covered furniture and an immense
dead clock and a gilt mirror & two *very handsome* crimson vases

this is reality - bed, medicine bottle, medicine glass marked
with tea and table spoons - guiacol tablets, balimanate of zinc

the *ancien couteau* burns faintly in my left lung tonight
you are so grown into my heart we are like the two wings of one bird

I look in the glass & am frightened of that girl with burning eyes
the wind sighs in the house and the fire goes *chik-chik* – very small –

how tired the dice get of being rattled and thrown

Maintenance

After Louise Bourgeois

The room seems to tilt,
unsteady to its core,

as a stainless knife
excises the windows.

She sanctioned replacement
but starts at the gasp

of the tripartite bay,
open to air.

All its mouths are agape -
a return to the moment

of birth, the fresh-peeled
cry of the body.

The faults in the glass snagged
like a twitch in the eyelid:

femme maison,
must she love what is meant

to improve her?
Her breath on the pane,

how it melted
the build-up of ice

in the bleakest of dawns.
The gaze from outside,

the gaze from within.
And the loss

of all of that looking.
Now she is tight,

laminate-muffled,
crisp in her finish.

She opens and shuts.
She fits in the frame.

She plugs up nostalgia,
its hurricane rattlings,

its whispers and shrieks,
and kills, for a while, what is cold.

Working Order

The issue concerned the bathroom window. Bare patches on the frame allowed steam to penetrate and to evaporate. When the air grew steamy after her bath, the frame grew tighter, and the window could not be opened without effort. When effort was applied, success of a kind was achieved. The window swung open but could no longer be closed. His skills lay in carpentry, he had paneled the kitchen ceiling in pine, he had boxed in the boiler in yellow pine, he had constructed a tiny room for the cot in a corner of their own bedroom from pine. She wanted him to apply these skills to the window, to plane and to sand, to seal and to paint. The window, she said. Well, do you want it open or closed, he said. It still came as a surprise that she wanted both.

The Voyage Out

After your slow
deliberation,
your incremental
gathering of pace,
after immersed
practice – drawing
watery breaths,
opening your eyes
on red dark –
after inward
concentration
on the growth
of each pleated,
delicate structure,
lungs folded flat,
voice-box airtight,
each gain propelled
by the umbilical pump
delivering oxygen
from belly to belly,
after all this
your chest is compressed
by the tunnel which leads
into cold blue light,
and out of the darkness
you eventually speed,
and all in one breath
you cry out the switch
from water to land
and plunge into air,
the horizon between
your sea and the sky
now available to
your salt-rinsed eyes.

The Airbnb's Backstory comes to Light

Late afternoon, a sun-baked breeze
blows constant from Mont Ventoux
across the valley to this washing line,
a plastic wire on flaking metal posts
above cherry orchards.

At the bottom of my basket
crumpled girls and boys collapse
against each other's chests;
I lift one, dripping of the city

and I pin consumptive children,
mouths turning to the mountain's kiss of life.
I squeeze water from their skinny limbs
and usher wind to ventilate their tissues,
contract and snap them back to supple shapes,
until they ripple, dance and flutter,
unpeg themselves and fly across the hill –

and, persuaded by air and space and sunlight,
I tell myself that this was all it took.
I try to see them gathered,
their bounce tucked up, delivered safely home,
as easy to restore to form and function
as wrung-out toweling, on an August afternoon.

Breathalia III

bronchi

branching
twins   conduct me
your non-identical
shapes adjust for sap   make space for
               the heart

Mirror

I discovered I was a pleated thing
chest tight as the coat of a bud
a winter instinct

a Fortuny dress laid flat on the bed
aligned and contained
silent in the absence of body

I couldn't place any melody
was I holding a voice in the folds
stitched to my spine

I only allowed a shallow inhale
child of depletion, child of compression
take a breath, little crow

crash through the glass

Did You Think You Could Relax?

I am thinking of felling the palm tree,
it nourishes nothing.

Its split trunk shivers beneath
a hairy blanket of matting.

Last year's yellowed spikes direct
drizzle at random angles,

but really what irritates most
is its bloody-mindedness.

Every year a new corona of fronds
brushes the obsolete telephone wire.

Don't tell me it's ornamental.
Don't tell me not to hack.

Vital Capacity

*Def: the maximum amount of air exhaled
after taking the deepest of breaths*

In this game, the ball's your breath
and the object is to get it out.

Each exhalation is a drive;
a silent partner lobs it back.

Can you reach the service line,
hit a deep shot to the back court?

Make it harder – add the tramlines
although there's only you to volley.

Draw it down until you gasp
and settle for a blocked return,

wary of your shortened action,
bronchi whistling at the ace.

Unfold your lungs and lay them flat.
They'd cover half a tennis court.

Inviolate

Violet isolates herself, or is isolated, tethered anchorite. The safest form of isolation is a negative-pressure room, where the air pressure inside is lower than outside the door. Her zephyrs blow in but not out, quite silently, and she could almost forget that a mechanism creates this effect. The mechanism is set in an outer wall, tracheotomy-style. Violet seems to bloom in this snare, however austere the hospital pillow, however blank the decor, however underripe the heaped bowl of mirabelles. Rocking gently, she oscillates from solitaire to sermon, practises the dialect. The air does not feel any thinner inside, and indeed Violet is told that she will find it no different at all. At intervals, she swallows clear soup. She is told that she cannot have a fan, for the air pressure in the room could be affected and blow infection under the door. Influx or reflux? The precepts are unclear. Can she presume to jut her lip, exhale hard enough to push her fringe from her eyes? Each out-breath hardens to an upswept plume, a blown-glass prayer. Violet interleaves tissue between each breakable breath, closets her whispers, preserves some positive evidence.

Breathalia IV

bronchioli

inside
your narrowing
stems   you sweep me along
pulled in with each gasp   discerning
                each note

Ghazal: April Inhalations

Patternless days, the park's winnowing my lockdown.
Apple blossom spirals, following the lockdown.

Leaflets, singing green, shield each apple bud
from frost or airborne blight, blowing in the lockdown.

The count is rising, the pollen and the bodies.
Each news report's a fractal, shadowing the lockdown.

Slower global rhythms sound a single tone,
a wasp tasked with surveillance, yellowing the lockdown.

Today, I miss the blackbird. Mess of feathers, silent nest.
Which animals are equal, undergoing lockdown?

Even language seems infected. This little suffix *-al*
— *viral, exponential* — is exploding in the lockdown.

To name myself, my love, would carve the page like stone.
A petal-blown memorial, the harrowing of the lockdown.

Confluence

The river's foundering

below its flooded bloat, it struggles to limit
itself, to reclaim its brink

from byways, meadows, homes it's overwhelmed

you've seen the aerial bulletins
and go down to gawp, join bystanders on a raised path

relatives at a bedside, where illness engulfs
familiar features

half-submerged, alder and willow
trace the banks

sweet iris blows in algaed sketches
on the towpath's board
mired in a phlegm of plastic bags

you could credit the old belief
that contagion lies in vapour,
blight in the drizzle you inhale

for now, it seems the planes are unaffected
contrails drift apart, diffusing into weather

Resurrecting the Author

For Barthes, the lung was *a stupid organ,*
lights for cats, fit only as offal
for *it swells but gets no erection.*

Let me unfold a lung, and begin.
Sans the fuel of the breath,
what use is a fine-grained larynx?

Plus that epithet *stupid* –
are you three years old, Roland,
stamping, declaring you are the man?

I'm on the back foot with you,
no theoretician,
so allow me my cursory skimming,

my Wiki – which I'd say you'd adore,
where truth lies with the editing reader
every text is eternally written here and now.

This matter of breath –
Barthes, you signal the death
of all but the words,

want me to discard
biographical context,
to interpret the language alone.

But this reader absorbs, and cannot
forget, your tubercular scars,
your fatherlessness

and reads into your throwaway lines
a great letting down
of unreliable organs, vulnerable flesh.

Breathalia V

alveoli

tiny
blooms transpire   held
on pedicels   my breath's
end and beginning   a lifespan
                your psalm

Notes

p.11   Italicised words in stanza two are from Keats' 'Ode to a Nightingale.' Keats died from TB in 1821 at the age of 25.

p.14   'How to Ration New Medication' is formed from advice given by Dr F C Edwards in *Tubercle 43 (1962) Suppl. 49*

p.16   'Breathe on me, breath of God' is a hymn traditionally sung at ordination.

p.13   'This is not a letter …' is a cento, drawn from Katherine Mansfield's letters to John Middleton Murry. Mansfield died from TB in 1923 at the age of 34.

p.33   Italicised words are from Roland Barthes' essays 'The Grain of the Voice' and 'The Death of the Author.' Barthes survived TB but died of chest injuries in 1980 at the age of 64 after a traffic accident.

Acknowledgements

My thanks to the editors of these journals and anthologies where some of these poems or versions of them have been published: *Stand, New Boots and Pantisocrasies, The High Window, The Honest Ulsterman, Bedford Square 10, Acumen, Tentacular*. 'Ghazal: April Inhalations' was shortlisted for the Bridport Prize.

Special thanks to Aaron Kent and Broken Sleep Books, my Corrupted Pedants, Kathryn Maris and Rebecca Goss. All my love as ever to Ed, Rob, Alex and James.

BREATHE OUT YOUR UNREST

Lightning Source UK Ltd.
Milton Keynes UK
UKHW020626080222
398338UK00006B/68